A DINOSAUR'S DAY

Stegosaurus
MAKES ITS WAY HOME

DK

MARIE BOLLMANN
ELIZABETH GILBERT BEDIA

Rugged. Resilient. Resourceful.

This is Stegosaurus.
Her name means "plated lizard."

Join this herbivore as she munches
her way through an adventure-filled
day in the Jurassic.

Ready or not, here we go!

As the hazy sun peeks over the horizon, little Stegosaurus wakes up from her slumber.

She stretches her short
trunk-like legs, arches her
plated back, and flexes
her spiky tail.

All around her, there are stegosauruses...

Little ones.

Big ones.

And ones of every size in between.

Her herd is waking up to a
new day, and so are...

Rumble. Grumble.

Rumble. Grumble.

...their tummies.

Little Stegosaurus and her herd are hungry.

They Munch, Munch, Munch on juicy ferns,
crunchy cycads, and waxy ginkgo trees, as
they wander at the edge of the forest.

Other plant-eating herds wander and munch, too.

Brachiosaurus.

Camptosaurus.

Diplodocus.

Stegosaurus uses her sharp
toothless beak to...

Snip, Tear, Chew

Snip. Tear. Chew
She savors each tasty bite.

Until, the ground
begins to **shake**...

Boom!

Boom! Boom!

Ceratosaurus is on the hunt for his own
breakfast. His golden eyes focus on the
slow-moving Stegosaurus herd.

He charges as his razor-sharp teeth get ready to...

Chomp!

The Stegosaurus herd circles together to protect the smaller dinosaurs, as the larger ones prepare for a battle.

Stegosauruses might not be as fast
or as crafty as Ceratosaurus, but
they are **rugged** and **resilient**.

Wielding their flexible, daggered tails, two giant Stegosauruses strike Ceratosaurus. **Resourceful**.

Kapow!

Kapow!

Ooouuuch!

Though injured, Ceratosaurus lets out a **GRUNT** and charges at the herd again. When...

A giant **BA-BOOM** hurtles through the air! Is it another dinosaur? No! It's a **HUGE** thunderstorm!

Boom!
Boom!

Flash!

C-R-A-C-K!

As a lightning bolt strikes the ground, Ceratosaurus retreats and the herds of dinosaurs scatter.

In all the chaos, little Stegosaurus loses sight of her herd.

After some time, the rain slows, and
Stegosaurus spots some muddy footprints.

Little ones.

Big ones.

And ones of every size in between.
They lead to a cave...

Stegosaurus lets out a **cry** in the cave.
A low **RUM-M-B-B-L-L-L-E** answers her.

Could it be her herd?
She wanders closer
and closer.

NO! It's a sleeping **Allosaurus**.
YIKES!

One day, Stegosaurus will be a tough opponent
for Allosaurus, thanks to her protective
scales, spiky tail, and armored plates.

But for now, she **sneaks** away!

Shhhhh,

As Stegosaurus steps out into the late afternoon sun she begins to feel sleepy.

She **MOPES** and **wanders**, until she stumbles across her favorite tasty treat—ginkgo nuts!

Stegosaurus hears **Munching** behind her. Could it be...

Her herd!

They love ginkgo nuts, too.

It has been an adventure-filled day!

With the full moon on the rise, Stegosaurus curls up by her herd and **finally** falls asleep.

Who was Stegosaurus?

Stegosaurus was a herbivore, which meant it ate plants for food.

Stegosaurus had large bony plates running along its back.

Stegosaurus was about the size of an elephant, but its brain was the size of an apple!

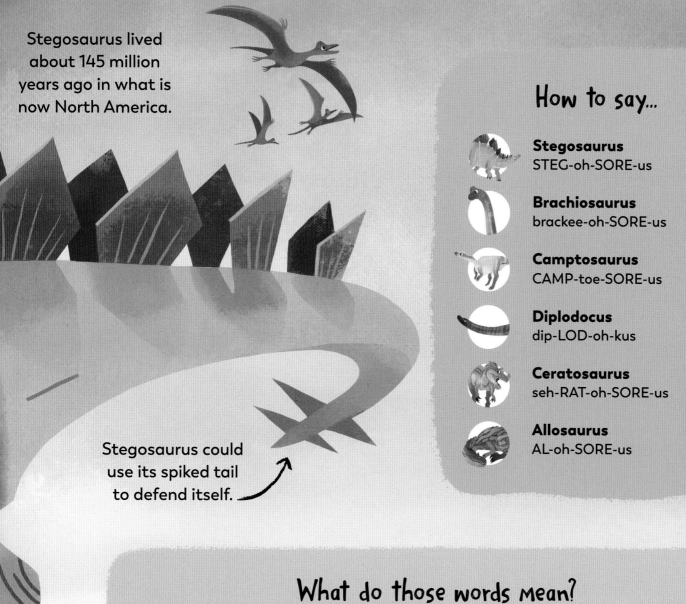

Stegosaurus lived about 145 million years ago in what is now North America.

Stegosaurus could use its spiked tail to defend itself.

How to say...

Stegosaurus
STEG-oh-SORE-us

Brachiosaurus
brackee-oh-SORE-us

Camptosaurus
CAMP-toe-SORE-us

Diplodocus
dip-LOD-oh-kus

Ceratosaurus
seh-RAT-oh-SORE-us

Allosaurus
AL-oh-SORE-us

What do those words mean?

Jurassic
The second of the three time periods when dinosaurs lived.

Herd
A group of animals that lives and travels together.

Herbivore
An animal that eats plants for food.

Fern
A leafy plant that was eaten by lots of dinosaurs.

Cycad
A type of plant common when dinosaurs lived.

Ginkgo
One of the oldest types of trees.

About the illustrator

Marie Bollmann is an illustrator who specializes in children's books. Marie was born in Münster, Germany, and is now based in Hamburg. She likes creating colorful, detailed illustrations, and her favorite dinosaur is Triceratops.

About the author

Elizabeth Gilbert Bedia is a former teacher and audiologist. She loves creating stories about our amazing world. She is the author of *Bess the Barn Stands Strong*, and *Balloons for Papa*. She lives in central Iowa with her dinosaur-loving family. You can visit her at www.elizabethgilbertbedia.com.

About the consultant

Dougal Dixon is a Scottish paleontologist, geologist, author, and educator. He has written more than 100 books, including the seminal work of speculative biology *After Man*, and award-winning *When the Whales Walked*.

Illustrator Marie Bollmann
Text for DK by Elizabeth Gilbert Bedia & Et Al Creative

Senior Acquisitions Editor James Mitchem
US Senior Editor Shannon Beatty
Senior Art Editor Charlotte Bull
Editor Rea Pikula
Design Assistant Sif Nørskov
Consultant Dougal Dixon
Jacket and Sales Material Coordinator Elin Woosnam
Senior Production Editor Nikoleta Parasaki
Senior Production Controller Ben Radley
Deputy Art Director Mabel Chan
Publishing Director Sarah Larter

First American Edition, 2024
Published in the United States by DK Publishing
1745 Broadway, 20th Floor, New York, NY 10019

A catalog record for this book
is available from the Library of Congress.
ISBN: 978-0-7440-9825-9

DK books are available at special discounts when purchased
in bulk for sales promotions, premiums, fund-raising,
or educational use. For details, contact:
DK Publishing Special Markets,
1745 Broadway, 20th Floor, New York, NY 10019
SpecialSales@dk.com

Printed and bound in China

www.dk.com

MIX
Paper | Supporting
responsible forestry
FSC™ C018179

This book was made with Forest
Stewardship Council™ certified
paper – one small step in DK's
commitment to a sustainable future.
For more information go to
www.dk.com/our-green-pledge